Taste

First published in the U.S. in 1994 by Carolrhoda Books, Inc.
c/o The Lerner Group
241 First Avenue North, Minneapolis, Minnesota 55401

Copyright © 1993 Wayland (Publishers) Ltd., Hove, East Sussex
First published 1993 Wayland (Publishers) Ltd.

Library of Congress Cataloging-in-Publication Data

Suhr, Mandy.
    Taste / written by Mandy Suhr ; illustrated by Mike Gordon.
        p.   cm. – (I'm alive)
    Originally published: Wayland Publishers, 1993.
    ISBN 0-87614-836-4
    1. Taste–Juvenile literature. [1. Taste. 2. Senses and
sensation.] I. Gordon, Mike, ill. II. Title. III. Series: Suhr, Mandy.
I'm alive.
QP456.S84 1994   93-44191
612.8′7–dc20   CIP
                                                        AC

Printed in Italy by Rotolito Lombarda S.p.A., Milan
Bound in the United States of America

1 2 3 4 5 6 – P/OS – 99 98 97 96 95 94

Taste

written by Mandy Suhr
illustrated by Mike Gordon

Carolrhoda Books, Inc.
Minneapolis

Look inside this store. All these
foods have different tastes.

What do you think
they might taste like?

Some things taste sweet.

Some things taste salty.

Some things taste sour…

or bitter.

Some foods taste really good when they are eaten together.

You should never taste something if you are not sure what it is. It might be poisonous.

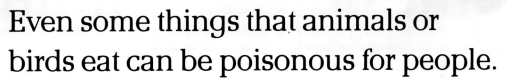

Even some things that animals or birds eat can be poisonous for people.

You use your tongue to taste things.

Inside your tongue are lots of tiny taste detectors. These are called taste buds.

When you put food into your mouth, the taste buds on different parts of your tongue detect different kinds of tastes.

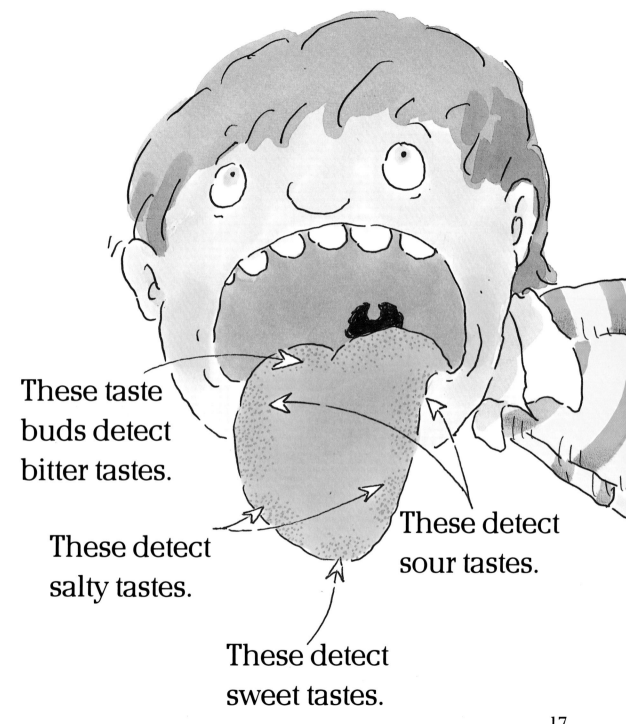

These taste buds detect bitter tastes.

These detect salty tastes.

These detect sour tastes.

These detect sweet tastes.

17

Your tongue can also tell you
whether foods are cold...

or hot...

and what they feel like.

All your senses work together, but smell and taste are special partners. When you smell something, it helps you to guess what the taste will be like.

If you have a cold and your nose is blocked, then you can't smell or taste things very well.

Most animals also have a sense of
taste. Some have taste buds.

But many animals have other ways
of tasting things. Flies can taste
with their feet!

Some animals are very fussy
about the taste of their food...

but others don't seem to
care about it at all!

What are your favorite tastes?

Ask an adult to help you and your friends play this taste game. Can your friends guess what each food is just by tasting it?

Now hold your nose. Can you still
guess what each food is by tasting it?

A note to adults

"I'm Alive" is a series of books designed especially for preschoolers and beginning readers. These books look at how the human body works and develops. They compare the human body to plants, animals, and objects that are already familiar to children.

Here are some activities that use what kids already know to learn more about their sense of taste.

Activities

1. Make a poster of tastes. Take a sheet of construction paper and draw a line down the middle. Label one side "tastes I like" and the other side "tastes I don't like." Then look through old magazines for pictures of foods that you like or don't like. Cut out the pictures and paste them on the construction paper. Show your poster to other people and ask what they think of your choices. You may find that something that tastes great to you tastes terrible to someone else!

2. The next time your mother or father is making dinner, pull up a chair and watch. Notice what it is that gives each dish a special flavor. Perhaps it is a certain spice or a special kind of cheese. If you're lucky, you may even get a taste.

3. Try a food you've never tasted before. Do you like the taste? Why or why not? Can you think of other foods that taste like this one? If you try enough new foods, you're sure to find some new favorites.

4. Make a list of your favorite foods. Think about the taste of each food. Is it salty, like pretzels or potato chips? Is it sweet, like cookies or ice cream? Maybe it's spicy, like pizza or tacos. Is there one taste you seem to like best?

Titles in This Series